ABCs AND OTHER LEARNING RHYMES

SELECTED BY SALLY EMERSON
ILLUSTRATED BY MOIRA & COLIN MACLEAN

BCA

LONDON   NEW YORK   SYDNEY   TORONTO

This edition published 1992 by BCA by arrangement with
Kingfisher Books, Grisewood & Dempsey Ltd,
Elsley House, 24–30 Great Titchfield Street, London W1P 7AD

The material in this edition was previously published by Kingfisher Books in
The Kingfisher Nursery Treasury (1988), *The Kingfisher Playtime Treasury* (1989)
and *The Kingfisher Nursery Treasure Chest* (1991).

CN 1903

Printed and bound in Spain

CONTENTS

A was an apple pie

B bit it

C cut it

D dealt it

E enjoyed it

F fought for it

G got it

H had it

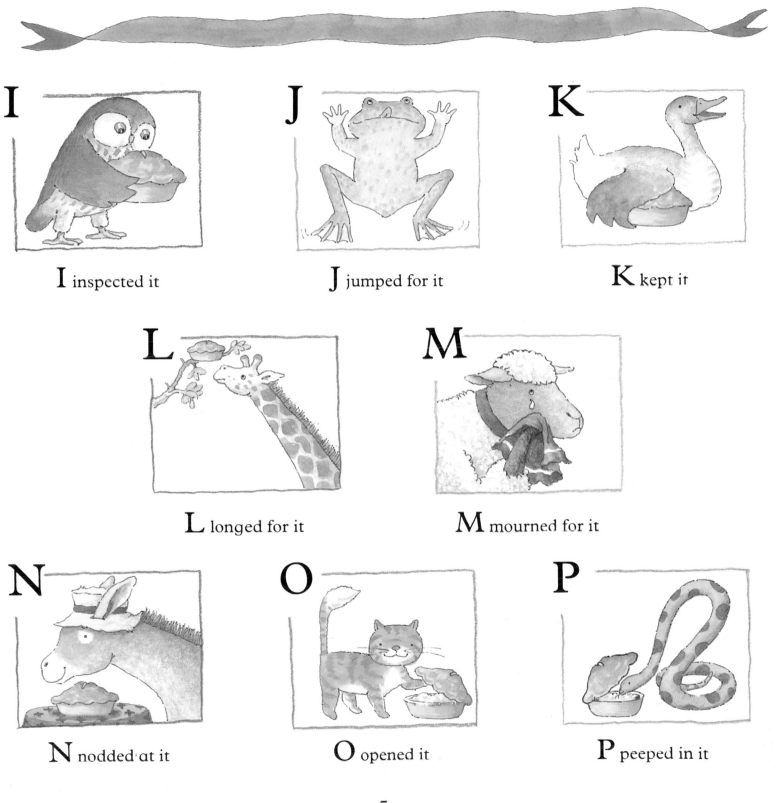

I inspected it

J jumped for it

K kept it

L longed for it

M mourned for it

N nodded at it

O opened it

P peeped in it

5

Q

Q quartered it

R

R ran for it

S

S sang for it

T

T took it

U

U upset it

V

V viewed it

W

W wanted it

XYZ

XYZ and & all wished
for a piece in hand

Bow-wow, says the dog,
Mew, mew, says the cat,
Grunt, grunt, goes the hog,
And squeak goes the rat.
Tu-whu, says the owl,
Caw, caw, says the crow,
Quack, quack, says the duck,
And what cuckoos say you know.

cuckoo!

One, two, three, four, five,
  Once I caught a fish alive,
Six, seven, eight, nine, ten,
  Then I threw it back again.
Why did you let it go?
  Because it bit my finger so.
Which finger did it bite?
  This little finger on the right.

1, 2, 3, 4,
  Mary at the kitchen door.
5, 6, 7, 8,
  Counting cherries off a plate.

Tinker,
Tailor,
Soldier,
Sailor,
Rich man,
Poor man,
Beggar man,
Thief.

Lady,
Baby,
Gipsy,
Queen.
This year,
Next year,
Sometime,
Never.

One little elephant went out one day,
Upon a spider's web to play;
He had such tremendous fun,
He sent for another elephant to come.

Two little elephants went out one day,
Upon a spider's web to play;
They had such tremendous fun,
They sent for another elephant to come.

Three little elephants went out one day,
Upon a spider's web to play;
They had such tremendous fun,
They sent for another elephant to come *etc*.

*Choose someone to be the first elephant. He walks around
swinging one arm like an elephant's trunk. At the end of the
verse the first elephant chooses a second elephant who holds on
to him with her "trunk". Continue until everyone is an elephant!*

One's none,
Two's some,
Three's many,
Four's a penny,
Five's a little hundred.

Five little speckled frogs
Sat on a speckled log
Eating the most delicious bugs –
Yum, yum.
One jumped into the pool
Where it was nice and cool,
Then there were four more speckled frogs.
Glub, glub!

Verses
Four little speckled frogs *etc.*
Three little speckled frogs *etc.*
Two little speckled frogs *etc.*

One little speckled frog
Sat on a speckled log
Eating the most delicious bugs –
Yum, yum.
He jumped into the pool
Where it was nice and cool,
Now there are no more speckled frogs,
Glub, glub!

*Squat on the floor like frogs. One by one take
it in turns to be the frog that jumps into
the pool. Repeat the song each time, counting
down. Teddies and other toys make
good frogs if you haven't enough players.*

One, two,
Buckle my shoe;

Three, four,
Knock at the door;

Five, six,
Pick up sticks;

Seven, eight,
Lay them straight;

Nine, ten,
A big fat hen;

Eleven, twelve,
Dig and delve;

Thirteen, fourteen,
Maids a-courting;

Fifteen, sixteen,
Maids in the kitchen;

Seventeen, eighteen,
Maids in waiting;

Nineteen, twenty,
My plate's empty.

*Both of these rhymes can be played
with five children or toys.*

There were five in the bed and
the little one said: Roll over! Roll over!
So they all rolled over and one fell out.

There were four in the bed *etc*.
There were three in the bed *etc*.
There were two in the bed *etc*.

There was one in the bed,
And that little one said:
Good, now I've got the bed to myself, I'm going to
stretch and stretch and stretch!

Five brown teddies sitting on a wall,
Five brown teddies sitting on a wall,
And if one brown teddy should accidentally fall,
There'd be four brown teddies sitting on a wall.

Sing to the tune of
"Ten Green Bottles".

Four brown teddies sitting on a wall *etc.*
Three brown teddies sitting on a wall *etc.*
Two brown teddies sitting on a wall *etc.*
One brown teddy sitting on a wall,
And if one brown teddy should accidentally fall,
There'd be no brown teddies sitting there at all!

A was an archer and shot at a frog;

B was a butcher and had a great dog.

C was a captain, all covered with lace;

D was a drummer and had a red face.

E was an esquire with pride on his brow;

F was a farmer and followed the plough.

G was a gamester who had but ill-luck;

H was a hunter and hunted a buck.

 **I** was an innkeeper who loved to carouse;

 **J** was a joiner and built up a house.

K was a king, so mighty and grand;

L was a lady and had a white hand.

 **M** was a miser and hoarded up gold;

 **N** was a nobleman, gallant and bold.

O was an oyster girl and went about town;

P was a parson and wore a black gown.

Q was a queen
who wore
a silk slip;

R was a robber
and wanted
a whip.

S was a sailor
and spent all
he got;

T was a tinker
and mended
a pot.

U was a usurer,
a miserable
elf;

V was a vintner
who drank all
himself.

W was a watchman
and guarded
the door;

X was expensive
and so became
poor.

Y was a youth
and did not
love school;

Z was a zany,
a poor
harmless fool.

Thirty days hath September,
April, June, and November;
All the rest have thirty-one,
Excepting February alone;
And that has twenty-eight days clear
And twenty-nine in each leap year.

Mr East gave a feast;
Mr North laid the cloth;
Mr West did his best;
Mr South burnt his mouth
With eating a cold potato.

The cock does crow
To let you know
If you be wise
'Tis time to rise;
For early to bed
And early to rise
Is the way to be healthy
And wealthy and wise.

See a pin and pick it up,
All the day you'll have good luck.
See a pin and let it lay,
Bad luck you'll have all the day.

Red sky at night,
   Shepherd's delight;
Red sky in the morning,
   Shepherd's warning.

Mackerel sky,
Mackerel sky,
Not long wet
And not long dry.

Manners in the dining-room,
  Manners in the hall,
If you don't behave yourself
  You shan't have none at all.

A wise old owl sat in an oak,
The more he heard the less he spoke;
The less he spoke the more he heard,
Why aren't we all like that wise old bird?

Go to bed late,
Stay very small;
Go to bed early,
Grow very tall.

Monday's child
is fair of face,

Tuesday's child
is full of grace.

Wednesday's child
is full of woe,

Thursday's child
has far to go,

Friday's child
is loving and giving,

Saturday's child
works hard for its living,

And the child that's born on the Sabbath day
Is bonny and blithe, and good and gay.

INDEX OF FIRST LINES